HYGGE NATURE

SUPER CUTE AND FUN ADULT COLORING BOOK

Hygge (pronounced "hyoo-guh"), a Danish art of coziness and contentment, is deeply connected to nature's tranquility. Whether it is the warmth of sunlight, the rustle of leaves, or the vibrant colors of wildflowers in full bloom, nature creates the perfect setting for slowing down and savoring simple pleasures. This bond inspires **HYGGE NATURE** coloring book, where cute animal characters enjoy Hygge moments surrounded by beautiful flowers, inviting you to join them in relaxing and reconnecting with nature's soothing charm.

THIS BOOK BELONGS TO

BEFORE YOU START...

Dear Creative Maestros,

To ensure the best coloring experience, please consider the following tips:

- The paper in this book is well-suited for colored pencils.

- If you are using alcohol-based markers, to prevent any bleed-through and protect the page underneath, we recommend placing a piece of thick paper or card stock behind the paper you are coloring.

This simple step will help keep the rest of your book clean and ensure your artwork remains pristine.

Happy Coloring !

Use Blank Thick Sheet of Paper
or
Use Card Stock

TEST COLOR PAGE

SHARE WITH US

We would love to see your amazing coloring creations!

Share your beautiful masterpiece on **Instagram** and **Tik Tok**, and tag us **@SuiSui_Coloring**. Whether you are bringing to life the cozy scenes or adding vibrant flair to the pages, we can't wait to feature and celebrate your work. Use the tag **#SuiSui_Coloring** for chance to be featured in our stories and posts.

Join the fun in our **Facebook** group: **Sui Sui Coloring Community**, where you can connect, share, and be inspired. Let's spread Creativity and Love together!

Instagram QR Code

Facebook Group QR Code

Tik Tok QR Code

FREE BONUSES FOR YOU

Dear Creative Maestros,

We know how much joy coloring brings. If you don't want the fun to stop and if you have finished this book but you are not ready to part with this Super Cute and Fun Creatures yet, we've got **Free Bonuses For You**.

What Do You Get for Free?
- Additional Coloring pages with Super Cute and Fun Creatures
  BONUS 1: $~~10.00~~ - **FREE 8+ pages**
  BONUS 2: $~~15.00~~ - **FREE 35+ pages**
  BONUS 3: $~~15.00~~ - **FREE 35+ pages**
  BONUS 4: $~~15.00~~ - **FREE 34+ pages**
  Total: ~~$55.00~~ - **FREE 112+ pages**
- Extended Enjoyment and Fun to keep your creativity buzzing

Use camera on your phone,
then Scan the code,
Click the Link

Where Do You Get the Free Bonuses?

https://suisuibooks.com/free-gift100   or

Happy Coloring!

SUI SUI

CAN WE ASK FOR A TINY FAVOR?

THANK YOU for picking up this book and joining me in this fun - artistic adventure.

If you have enjoyed our Coloring Book, we have a tiny favor to ask:

Could you please take moment right now and leave a review on Amazon?
It will only take less than **60 seconds**

Your feedback is incredibly valuable - it is like the lifeblood for a small independent author like me. By sharing your thoughts, you are contributing significantly to my publishing journey.

Your review will also help others discover the joy of coloring and support my work in a meaningful way. People do judge a book by its reviews. That **one minute** of your time can truly make a world of difference to me.

To leave the review:
   1. Pick 1x Amazon store where you purchased the book from:

USA
   UK

Canada

Australia

France.

Netherlands

   2. Use camera on your phone, Scan the Code, click the link, leave the review